DINOSAURS
AND THEIR WORLD

PAUL HARRISON and HEATHER AMERY

ARCTURUS

CONTENTS

THE BEGINNING

If you could see the earth when it first came into being, about 4.5 billion years ago, you would see little more than a ball of molten rock. It gradually cooled, rains fell and seas formed. It was in the seas that life began.

FIRST LIFE
The first living things were bacteria so small they were invisible to the naked eye. They produced oxygen and, over time, created an atmosphere in which other life forms could grow.

At Hamelin Pool in Australia there are living fossils called stromatolites. They began to form over 3 billion years ago and are still growing.

▲ WATERY WONDERS
After bacteria came simple animals such as sponges, jellyfish and trilobites. Trilobites were like underwater woodlice. They flourished for nearly 300 million years despite never growing bigger than 70 cm (2 ft). They vanished from the seas about 250 million years ago.

▲ LATE DEVELOPER

The first fish appeared over 500 million years ago. Within 100 million years, bigger creatures were terrorizing the seas. Dunkleosteus (dunk-lee-OWE-stee-us) was a super-predator at over 10 m (33 ft) long. The first sharks appeared then, too.

◄ NOT SO FUNNY

One of the earliest predators was a strange creature called Anomalocaris (a-nom-uh-lo-CARE-is). It was the scourge of the seas over 500 million years ago. It looked like a large shrimp but with a trunk-like arm next to its mouth for catching prey.

ON LAND

One of the reasons animals evolve is to adapt to new places. Some creatures left the crowded seas to escape predators. They adapted to life on land.

IT'S A MYSTERY

The first animal to venture onto land remains a mystery. Scientists believe it must have been able to breathe air as well as live under water. Some people think a creature called Pederpes (peh-DER-pees) was the first to walk on the land. It lived around 350 million years ago.

PLANTS POP UP ▶

Plants appeared on earth over 400 million years ago, changing earth's atmosphere. Over the next few million years, plant life evolved from leafless shoots to huge forests.

BIG INSECTS ▶

Once the land had been conquered, creatures took to the air. Insects were the first to fly. Some species developed wings and evolved into the most impressive insects ever seen, such as dragonflies with wingspans of 70 cm (2 ft)!

An animal that can live on land and in water is called an amphibian.

▼ FINTASTIC

Reptiles evolved around 70 million years after the first land animals. Initially, they were quite small. One of the most ferocious was Dimetrodon (di-MET-ro-don). Like reptiles today, Dimetrodon would have been cold-blooded. It had a bony fin on its back that might have been used to absorb the sun's warmth.

Small reptiles evolved into some of the most impressive animals ever to walk the earth – the dinosaurs! Some were as small as chickens. Others were longer than three buses put together. From knee-high to sky-high, the dinosaurs ruled the earth for about 160 million years.

DINOSAUR DAYS

The earliest dinosaurs lived during the Triassic period (245–208 million years ago). Then came the Jurassic period (208–146 million years ago). After that was the Cretaceous period (146–65 million years ago), during which all the dinosaurs disappeared.

▼ EMPTY NESTERS

Like most reptiles, dinosaurs hatched from eggs. Some fossils show that certain dinosaurs may have been very protective of their young. The plant-eater Maiasaura (MY-ah-SAW-rah) guarded its babies and brought them food.

DOMINATED

Scientists believe that there are hundreds of dinosaur species yet to be found.

▼ DIG IT

When most dinosaurs died, their bodies just rotted away. But in the right conditions, the bones were preserved and turned to stone. These ancient remains are called fossils and it is by studying fossils that we know so much about dinosaurs.

What is it about dinosaurs that we find so fascinating? It's probably their size. Huge dinosaurs dominated the planet during the Triassic and Jurassic periods. Fierce carnivores (meat-eaters) lived side by side with giant herbivores (plant-eaters).

◄ HUNTERS AND HUNTED

As well as the huge herbivores, there were smaller plant-eaters that would have been a tasty snack for a hungry carnivore. Often they were fast and agile so they could outrun big, heavy carnivores.

GIANTS

Because some dinosaurs had nostrils on the top of their heads, it was once thought they lived in the water.

▼ LAND SPREAD

Before the early Jurassic period, the earth had just one land mass. Slowly, this broke up to make the continents we have today. As a result, remains of giant dinosaurs are found all over the world.

▼ HIP HOORAY

All dinosaurs were reptiles, but dinosaurs had their legs underneath, rather than at the sides like modern reptiles. The shape of the hip bones helps to show the connection between dinosaurs and their descendants, the birds.

MIGHTY MEAT-EA

Carnivorous dinosaurs were the most fearsome. Some were hunters and others were scavengers, but they all had the same favourite meal – MEAT. When their dagger-like, flesh-ripping teeth fell out, new ones grew to take their place, so even an old meat-eater had a killer bite.

◄ **RUN FOR YOUR LIFE!**
Some of the most dangerous dinosaurs were small but speedy. Deinonychus (die-NON-I-cus) was only 3 m (9 ft) long, but it was fast and fierce, with savage claws.

TERS

The great meat-eater Megalosaurus (MEG-ah-loh-SAW-rus) was the first dinosaur ever to be named.

▲ ARMED AND DANGEROUS

All of the top predators of the Jurassic period had sharp, jagged teeth, but many had other weapons too. Sharp claws could hold down prey and powerful tails could be used for defence.

We can find out what dinosaurs ate by studying fossils.

▼ AFRICAN GIANT

Carcharodontosaurus (car-KA-roh-DON-toh-SAW-rus) was one of the biggest carnivores in North Africa during the Cretaceous period. At around 14 m (46 ft), it was even longer than Tyrannosaurus rex (ty-RAN-oh-SAW-rus rex).

SMILE, PLEASE ▶

Carcharodontosaurus means 'shark-toothed lizard'. As this huge skull shows, it had a mouth full of very sharp teeth. It must have terrified the plant-eaters of its day.

SCARY ◄ SOUTHERNER

Giganotosaurus (jy-GAN-oh-toh-SAW-rus) has only recently been discovered in Argentina. It roamed South America in the middle Cretaceous period, about 90 million years ago, long before Tyrannosaurus rex was terrorizing North America.

HAIL TO THE KING! ▲

Tyrannosaurus rex is possibly the most famous of all giant dinosaur species. Around 6 m (20 ft) high, this massive meat-eater was taller than a double-decker bus and had teeth as long as bananas.

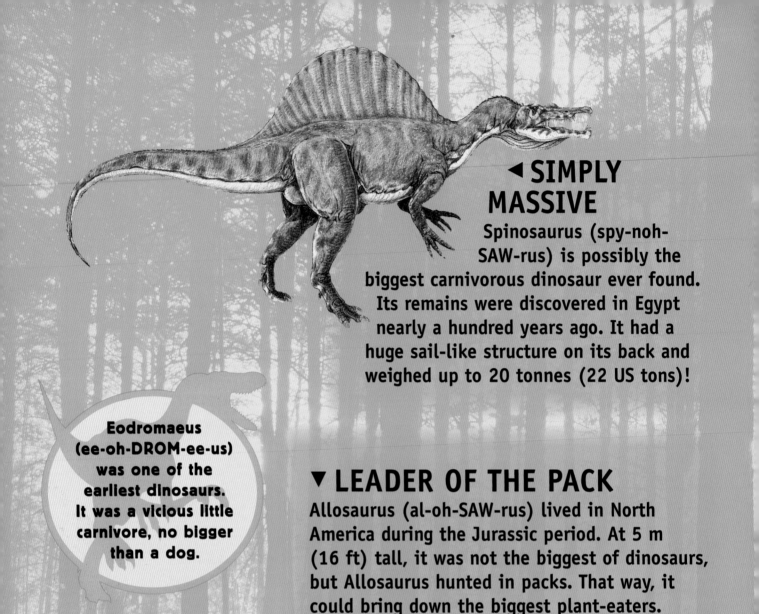

◀ SIMPLY MASSIVE

Spinosaurus (spy-noh-SAW-rus) is possibly the biggest carnivorous dinosaur ever found. Its remains were discovered in Egypt nearly a hundred years ago. It had a huge sail-like structure on its back and weighed up to 20 tonnes (22 US tons)!

Eodromaeus (ee-oh-DROM-ee-us) was one of the earliest dinosaurs. It was a vicious little carnivore, no bigger than a dog.

▼ LEADER OF THE PACK

Allosaurus (al-oh-SAW-rus) lived in North America during the Jurassic period. At 5 m (16 ft) tall, it was not the biggest of dinosaurs, but Allosaurus hunted in packs. That way, it could bring down the biggest plant-eaters.

▲FOOD FIGHTS

While some herbivores may have been gentle, they didn't give up without a struggle. In Mongolia's Gobi Desert, the bones of a meat-eating Velociraptor (vel-O-si-RAP-tor) and the bones of a plant-eating Protoceratops (pro-toh-SER-a-tops) were found together. The two had fought to the death.

19

HUGE HERBIVORES

The biggest dinosaurs of all were herbivores. They went looking for food, not trouble, so other dinosaurs had little to fear from them. There were small plant-eaters, too, but they often had good defences so they could fight back if attacked.

▼ SAFETY IN NUMBERS

Big dinosaurs such as Brachiosaurus (BRAK-ee-oh-SAW-rus) would have roamed around in herds, just like elephants do today. Together they could protect their young from predators.

▶ BIG IS BRILLIANT?

Being big and strong meant giant dinosaurs were relatively safe from attack. But they needed giant meals. If food was scarce, they could easily starve.

Surprisingly, most dinosaurs were vegetarians. About 70 per cent were herbivores and only 30 per cent were carnivores.

◀ NO GRASS HERE

There was no grass during the time of the dinosaurs. There were some other familiar plants though, including figs, ferns, conifers and sycamores.

VICIOUS VEGGIE ▼

Brachiosaurus was as heavy as a dozen elephants. It was too massive to move fast, but it could use its thick and powerful tail to keep off attackers.

The first herbivorous dinosaurs appeared in the late Triassic period. They thrived during the Jurassic period but died out in Cretaceous times.

▲ TALL ORDER

Brachiosaurus belonged to the sauropod family. At around 16 m (52 ft), it could reach the leaves of tall trees while other sauropods had to feed at much lower levels.

Brachiosaurus might have been able to rear up on its huge hind legs to crash down on its enemy. Ouch!

THE COMPLETE FOSSIL

For many years, Brachiosaurus was the largest dinosaur known. In terms of the largest complete fossil skeleton found, it is still the record breaker!

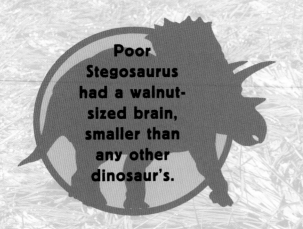

Poor Stegosaurus had a walnut-sized brain, smaller than any other dinosaur's.

▼ SPIKY FELLOW

The strange-looking Stegosaurus (STEG-oh-SAW-rus) was huge and weighed up to 7 tonnes (8 US tons), but it wasn't very quick. It defended itself with a strong, spiky tail. The spikes, some a metre (3 ft) long, could pierce the skin of any hungry predator.

◄ TOUGH LOVE

Pachycephalosaurus (PAK-ee-SEF-a-loh-SAW-rus) was a real bonehead! This plant-eater had a solid dome on the top of its skull that was 25 cm (10 in) thick. Scientists once believed it was for defence, but now they believe it was used in fights with other males during the mating season.

PLATE PUZZLER ▼

As well as a spiky tail, Stegosaurus had a row of triangular plates down its back. Palaeontologists (people who study prehistoric life) think it may have turned its plates towards the sun to soak up its warmth.

▼ HADROSAUR IN A HURRY

Edmontosaurus (ED-mon-toh-SAW-rus) belonged to the hadrosaur (HAD-roh-saw) family of dinosaurs. It lived in large herds in North America during the Cretaceous period. Over 13 m (42 ft) long and weighing around 3 tonnes (3 US tons), it could run as fast as a horse – handy for getting away from hungry carnivores.

Fossils of unknown dinosaur species are being discovered all the time. Around 40 per cent of all known species have been found in the last 20 years.

BACK OFF! ▶

Triceratops (try-SER-a-tops) looked a bit like a modern-day rhinoceros. It had three horns that were probably used for defence. It wouldn't have charged at its enemies. Its horns were only strong enough to be used as prodding weapons.

WRECKING BALL ▶

Ankylosaurus (an-KY-loh-SAW-rus) was armed and dangerous. Not only did it have spikes on its back, it had a rock-hard ball at the end of its tail to club any attackers.

27

# SOARING SAUROP

The biggest herbivores were a group called the sauropods (SAW-ro-pods). They had long necks and thick legs. They lived in herds and fed on huge quantities of vegetation.

Many plant-eating dinosaurs swallowed small rocks to help them digest their food.

▼ LOOKING DOWN

Diplodocus (di-PLOD-oh-cus) had short front legs making its head point downwards. This helped it to eat plants that grew low down on the ground, such as ferns.

▲ ARMOUR PLATED

At only 12 m (39 ft) in length, Saltasaurus (SALT-a-SAW-rus) was prey to the larger carnivores. Its defence was a covering of small bony plates that acted as a type of armour.

FUSSY
◄ EATER

Brachytrachelopan (BRAK-i-TRAK-eh-loh-pan) had an unusually short neck for a sauropod. The neck bones were joined together, limiting the movement of its head. It fed on vegetation 1–2 m (3–6 ft) above the ground.

▲ MISTAKEN IDENTITY

At 25 m long (82 ft), Brontosaurus (BRON-toh-SAW-rus) appeared to be a new dinosaur discovery. It turned out to be the already known Apatosaurus (A-PAT-oh-SAW-rus).

◄ SOME NECK

Sauropods were well known for their long necks. Just the neck of Mamenchisaurus (mah-MEN-chee-SAW-rus) measured 11 m (36 ft). That's the length of a bus!

RECORD BREAKERS

We know that some dinosaurs were big, but we don't know which was the biggest of all. Here are some contenders.

▲ MIGHTY MEAT MUNCHER

The biggest meat-eater is thought to be Spinosaurus, but it didn't feed on other dinosaurs. Its favourite food was fish.

Argentinosaurus (ar-gen-TEEN-oh-SAW-rus) was probably the heaviest. it may have weighed 100 tonnes (110 US tons)!

◄ LONG STRETCH

The record for the longest dinosaur discovered is held by Seismosaurus (syz-moh-SAW-rus) at an estimated 35 m (115 ft). Most of the length was neck and tail.

# FEARSOME FLIERS

In prehistoric times reptiles not only ruled the earth, they also filled the skies. The pterosaurs (TER-oh-SAWS) were flying reptiles with wings made of skin. Some were as small as birds, others were as big as aeroplanes!

The smallest pterosaur is thought to be the insect-eating Anurognathus (an-YOOR-og-NATH-us). Its wingspan was only 50 cm (20 in).

SUPER SCOOPER ▶

Pteranodon (te-RAN-oh-don) would skim over the water, scoop up fish, and swallow them whole, just like pelicans do today.

FEATHER ◄ FOSSIL

Archeopteryx (ark-ee-OP-ter-iks) is the first flying reptile known to have had feathery wings. It had claws on its wings too, which may have been used to climb trees.

◄ WINGING IT ►

At about 70 cm (2 ft) long, Microraptor (MY-cro-RAP-tor) was not big in dinosaur terms, but it had four wings. As well as its front wings, it had two feathery back legs that would help it to glide through the air.

▲ AIR-VOLUTION

Rhamphorynchus (RAM-foh-RING-cus), one of the early pterosaurs, had spiky teeth, ideal for spearing fish. Later flying reptiles like Quetzalcoatlus (kwet-zal-co-AT-lus) looked quite different. They had much shorter tails but longer necks.

FLAP OR GLIDE? ▶

An American scientist made a full-sized, remote-controlled, flying model of Quetzalcoatlus. He proved that the animal could have flapped its wings like a bird. Many believed it could only glide.

BIGGEST ◀ EVER?

Quetzalcoatlus is possibly the largest flying animal ever to be seen in the skies. With a wingspan of up to 12 m (39 ft), it was the size of a small aeroplane.

◄ CLAMMING UP

Dsungaripterus (JUN-gar-RIP-te-rus) had a beak that was made for prising clams apart. The flat teeth at the back of its beak could have been used for crushing the shells.

Odd as it may seem, the pterosaurs did not evolve into birds – the dinosaurs did.

BAT BIRD ►

Pteranodon had a crest on its head that may have helped it to steer in flight, like the tail fin on an aeroplane. But the crest may also have been used to attract a mate.

◀ LIGHTWEIGHT

Ornithocheirus (or-NITH-oh-KEE-rus) was another giant in the sky. It had a wingspan of up to 12 m (39 ft). In spite of its size, it was very lightweight because it had hollow bones.

OLD DEVIL ▶

Anhanguera (an-YANG-wear-ah) was a giant fish-eating pterosaur that lived in the Cretaceous period in Brazil. Its name means 'old devil'. It had no tail, which means it was an advanced pterosaur. The most advanced had no teeth either.

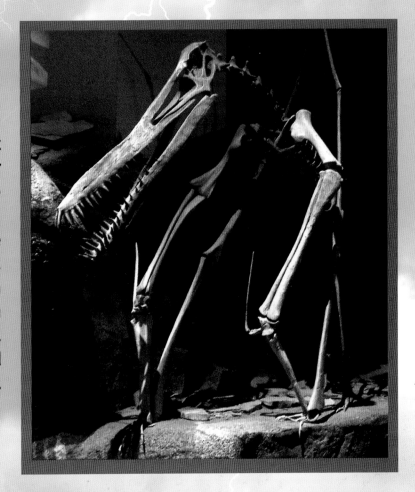

# REX RULED THE

When you hear the word 'dinosaur', which one comes to mind first? Bet you said Tyrannosaurus rex – one of the biggest, hungriest and fiercest of the meat-eating dinosaurs. Its name means 'king of the tyrant lizards'.

Palaeontology is the scientific name for the study of fossils.

END OF
◄ AN ERA
Tyrannosaurus rex was alive at the end of the reign of the dinosaurs. This was during the Cretaceous period. Scientists know more about this era than any other.

WORLD

CHANGING WORLD ▶

We know that continents move very slowly across the earth's surface. By Cretaceous times, what had once been a single landmass was breaking up and starting to form the continents we recognize today.

▼ BIG BOY

T. rex was the largest of the tyrannosaur family of dinosaurs that lived in North America around 85 to 65 million years ago.

FEARSOME FIND

There have been around 30 T. rex skeletons discovered in the world so far. An old, perfectly-preserved fossil attracts a lot of attention – and a lot of trouble.

▼ DINO DETECTIVE
Scientists like Jack Horner are hunting for T. rex fossils.

SUE FOR ◄ KEEPS
This fossil, nicknamed Sue, was discovered in 1990 in South Dakota, USA. A legal battle began about who owned the skeleton. In the end, the owner of the ranch where she was found was said to be the legal owner.

FEMME FATALE

Sue is the largest and most complete skeleton of a Tyrannosaurus rex ever found. She is now in the Field Museum in Chicago, USA.

SECOND PRIZE

The team who discovered Sue didn't get to keep her, but they have the skeleton of a T. rex called Stan, who was found two years after Sue.

Sue was named after the woman who found her, Sue Hendrickson.

▲ MOVING MONSTER

Visitors to London's Natural History Museum can get up close to a life-sized, animatronic model Tyrannosaurus rex.

THE EX-REX?

Everyone knows that T. rex was a top predator, but what was it really like? Was it as fearsome as it first appears? What did it eat? How fast could it run? What colour was it? People are still trying to answer these questions.

BIG AS A BUS ▶

T. rex measured over 12 m (3 ft) from nose to tail and was up to 6 m (20 ft) tall. It weighed more than an elephant.

It is thought that the female T. rex was bigger than the male.

SCALY ▲

T. rex had coarse, bumpy skin like an alligator. It would have felt like jagged stones. It was probably a dull colour so it could blend into the background, like predators do today.

THE NEW KING ▶

If T. rex and Giganotosaurus had lived in the same place at the same time, the Giganotosaurus might have been the tyrant king not T. rex. It was longer but no one knows if it was as fierce.

STRAIGHT TO THE

The huge size of Tyrannosaurus rex's head made it a terrifying dinosaur. Its mouth was packed full of scary, dangerous-looking teeth.

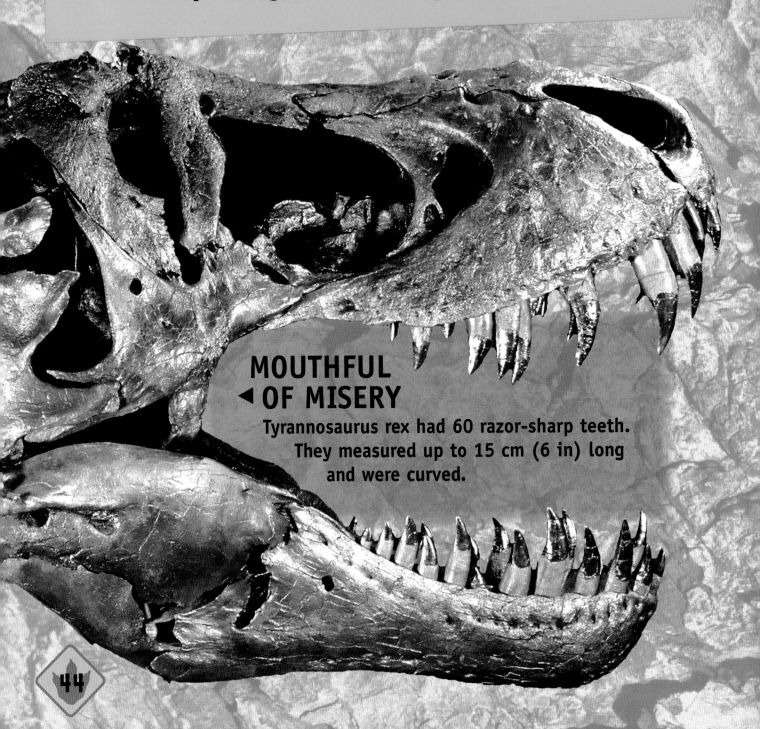

MOUTHFUL
◄ OF MISERY
Tyrannosaurus rex had 60 razor-sharp teeth. They measured up to 15 cm (6 in) long and were curved.

POINT

BIG BITE ▶

A T. rex's mouth was big enough to swallow a human whole and its teeth were strong enough to chomp through thick dinosaur bones.

T. rex was always growing new teeth to replace old or lost ones.

◀ SMALL ARMS

T. rex had very short, strong arms with two claws at the end. Scientists can't be sure what these arms were used for.

SAVAGE OR SCAV

Everyone agrees that Tyrannosaurus rex was a super-carnivore, but experts can't agree on whether it was a hunter or a scavenger. Scavengers eat animals that have already been killed, just like vultures and hyenas do today.

▲NOSY
Scavengers, such as vultures, can smell carrion (dead animals) from great distances. T. rex also had a good sense of smell.

HUNTER ▶
T. rex's strong head would have been useful for attacking other dinosaurs to eat them.

ENGER?

SLOWCOACH
T. rex probably had a top speed of no more than 40 kph (25 mph) – faster than a human, but pretty slow compared to other dinosaurs.

EYE CAN SEE YOU ▶
T. rex had forward-facing eyes just as many predators do today. Does this mean it was a hunter?

OVER TO YOU
Hunter or scavenger – what do you think? Perhaps T. rex was a bit of both.

The Cretaceous forest was a dangerous place for baby dinosaurs. They could be crushed by large plant-eating dinosaurs or eaten by other carnivores. They could even be eaten by one of their parents!

Even T. rex eggs were probably laid in a nest. It's unlikely they would have been sat on by their mother though!

▼HATCHING OUT

All dinosaurs would have started life in an egg. Some scientists think they covered their eggs in earth or leaves, like crocodiles do today.

PERFECT
◄ EGGS

The first and largest fossilized eggs were found in France in 1869. They were 30 cm (12 in) long and 25 cm (10 in) wide. The smallest dinosaur eggs ever found were only 2 cm (less than an inch) long. Some palaeontologists think T. rex's eggs may have been long and thin but, so far, none have been discovered.

PARENT
TROUBLE ►

Was T. rex a good parent? It is possible that female T. rexes may have hunted other dinosaurs to feed their young. However male T. rexes may have tried to kill and eat their own babies!

▲ GOING SOLO

It is generally believed that T. rex was a solitary dinosaur, because adult skeletons are usually found by themselves. Nobody really knows.

Some people believe that all dinosaurs had feathers. Can you imagine T. rex as a ferocious type of bird?

IN THE SEAS

While dinosaurs roamed the earth, equally awesome beasts ruled the seas. Some of these prehistoric sea monsters evolved from land reptiles and adapted to life in the water. They still had to come to the surface of the water to breathe between dives, like whales and dolphins do.

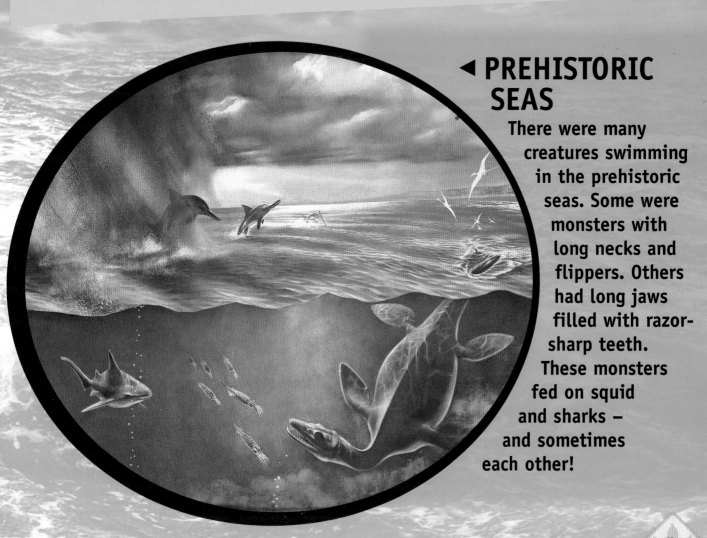

◄ PREHISTORIC SEAS

There were many creatures swimming in the prehistoric seas. Some were monsters with long necks and flippers. Others had long jaws filled with razor-sharp teeth. These monsters fed on squid and sharks — and sometimes each other!

◄ ANCIENT TERROR

Over 360 million years ago, the Dunkleosteus (dun-klee-OS-tee-us) was bigger and scarier than today's great white shark.

Fossils suggest that ichthyosaurs didn't lay eggs but gave birth to live young.

▼ DEADLY 'DOLPHIN'

Ichthyosaurs (IKH-thee-oh-saws) looked a lot like modern-day dolphins – but they were much, much bigger. They zipped through the water as fast as 40 kph (25 mph).

▲ DOWN IN THE DEPTHS

With their skinny necks and roly-poly bodies, plesiosaurs (PLE-see-oh-saws) looked awkward, but their paddle-like flippers helped them twist and turn in the water.

◀ MARINE MENACE

Liopleurodon (LIE-oh-PLOO-ro-don) was a ferocious predator. Its skull measured up to 3 m (10 ft) long and was full of sharp teeth.

PLESIOSAUR PREDATOR ▶

Kronosaurus (KRON-oh-SAW-rus) was a type of plesiosaur alive during the early Cretaceous period. It was around 12 m (39 ft) long and swam with four strong flippers.

LONG-NECKED ▶

Elasmosaurus (el-AS-moh-SAW-rus) was an extremely large plesiosaur. Up to 14 m (46 ft) long, half its length was neck.

Kronosaurus probably swam like a turtle – the biggest snapping turtle ever!

▼ OLD CROC

Sarcosuchus (SAR-koh-SOO-kiss) was a river-dwelling ancestor of today's crocodile. It ate fish but, at 13 m (43 ft) long, it was big enough to prey on dinosaurs coming to the river to drink.

GOING, GOING, GO

The dinosaurs ruled the earth for 165 million years. But 65 million years ago, they all disappeared. What happened? Did one catastrophic event wipe them out, or did they gradually become extinct?

▼VOLCANOES

Erupting volcanoes may have spewed out so much lava and poisonous gas into the air that the dinosaurs couldn't survive.

LIGHTS OUT ▶

A massive asteroid – more than 9 km (5 miles) wide – may have crashed down on earth, causing so much dust it blocked out the sun. The dinosaurs might have frozen in the cold!

There is another strange theory about what may have happened to the dinosaurs. Some people think that space aliens carried them away. What do you think?

COLD SPELL

A less dramatic explanation is that the earth's climate changed gradually. The weather got drier and cooler, and the dinosaurs just couldn't handle the chill.

▲ SHOWER OF DESTRUCTION

Whatever happened, there was so much debris in the air that, when it finally settled, it formed a layer in the rocks. This is known as the K/T boundary and can be found all over the world. Below this line there are dinosaur fossils. Above it, there are none.

HOLEY PROOF

A huge crater off the coast of Mexico suggests that an asteroid really did hit the earth years ago. The hole is called the Chicxulub crater and it is under the sea off the Yucatán Peninsula. It measures over 179 km (111 miles) across.

Scientists think the impact of the asteroid was a billion times more explosive than an atom bomb.

▲ FADING OUT

Dinosaurs had been decreasing in number for millions of years because the temperature was changing. They would have died out even if an asteroid had not hit the earth.

After the Dino

A question that still bothers palaeontologists is why dinosaurs disappeared but other animals, such as mammals, survived.

▼ EGG THIEVES

Some scientists think that mammals may have played a part in the extinction of the dinosaurs. After a meteor hit earth, small mammals may have reduced the number of dinosaurs even more by eating their eggs!

SAURS

FEATHERED
◄ FRIENDS

Most scientists now believe that birds have evolved from dinosaurs. Discoveries in China show that some baby dinosaurs may have had feathers to keep them warm.

Some dinosaurs breathed like birds, as the air went into tiny pouches in their lungs.

HOW WE KNOW

Everything we know about dinosaurs comes from the work of fossil-hunters, palaeontologists and other scientists. The newest technology is being used to try to find out even more.

RAINBOW COLOUR

Fossils tell us a great deal, but they can't tell us what colour the dinosaurs were. Palaeontologists look at animals today for clues. The colours of hunters, such as lions, usually blend with their backgrounds.

The only way palaeontologists can find out more about dinosaurs is if more fossils are found.

HARD ◄ WORK

Preparing fossils is slow work. It can take years to prepare a single fossil for display in a museum.

▼ WARM OR COLD?

Were dinosaurs warm- or cold-blooded? Dinosaurs were reptiles so they could have been cold-blooded but many scientists now believe that they were warm-blooded, like birds.

Tyrannosaurus rex (tie-ran-oh
Adult, full size.
Scavenger or predator?

Saurornitholestes (sore-or-nit
Adult, full size.
Definitely a killer!

◄ DIRTY JOB

Palaeontologists have to inspect dinosaur poo to discover what they ate. Fossilized poo is called coprolite.

EARLY MAMMALS

When the dinosaurs disappeared, so did over 50 per cent of all life. This was great news for mammals. The lack of competition for food and territory enabled mammals to grow and diversify.

A mammal is warm-blooded, which means it generates its own body heat – unlike a reptile.

MONKEYING AROUND ▶

Around 60 million years ago the first primates – apes and monkeys – evolved. The most complete remains found so far belong to Proconsul africanus (pro-CON-sul afri-KHAN-us), which lived around 18 million years ago. It walked on four legs and probably ate fruit.

GIDDY UP ▶

The first horses appeared over 40 million years ago. One of the most famous is Hyracotherium (high-rah-co-THEER-ee-um), often called the 'dawn horse'. It didn't look much like a horse – it didn't have hooves and was only 20 cm (8 in) high. Not great for riding, then!

Most mammals give birth to live young. However, some mammals, known as monotremes, lay eggs!

MARSUPIALS ▶

Marsupials are mammals that carry their new-born young in a pouch, just like kangaroos do today. The earliest may have appeared around 125 million years ago, so they would have rubbed shoulders with dinosaurs. They diverged into many different species.

UNDER WATER

Many sea reptiles went extinct at the end of the age of the dinosaurs. However, life in the water continued to thrive, producing all sorts of interesting creatures.

FLAT FISH ▼

Sharks are an evolutionary success story. Around during the time of the dinosaurs, they have diversified into other species. It is believed that rays evolved from sharks, adapting to life in shallow waters.

◄ SHELL-SHOCK

Turtles have been around for over 100 million years and some of them were huge. Archelon (ARK-eh-lon) lived alongside the dinosaurs and died out at the same time. It was about as big as a car.

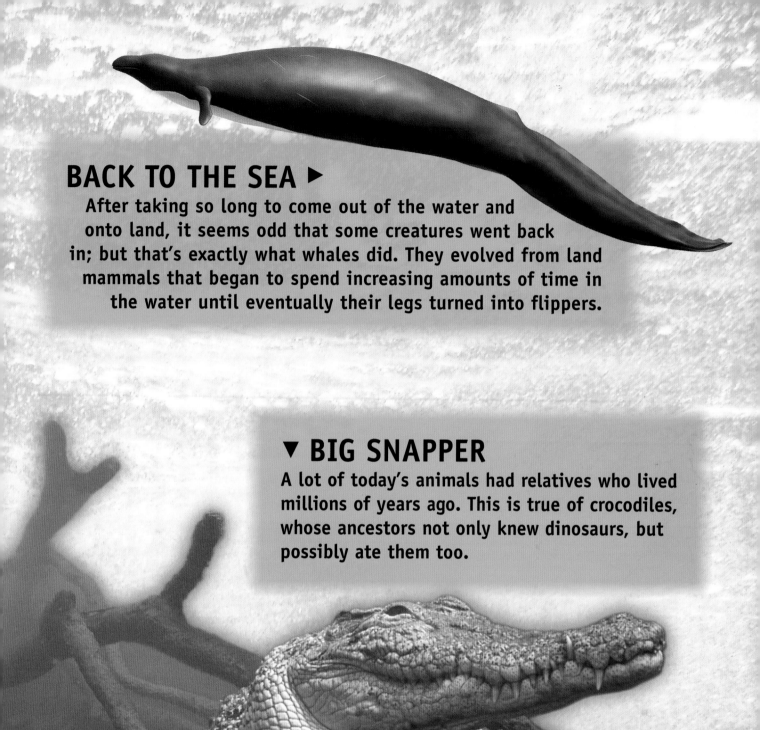

BACK TO THE SEA ▶

After taking so long to come out of the water and onto land, it seems odd that some creatures went back in; but that's exactly what whales did. They evolved from land mammals that began to spend increasing amounts of time in the water until eventually their legs turned into flippers.

▼ BIG SNAPPER

A lot of today's animals had relatives who lived millions of years ago. This is true of crocodiles, whose ancestors not only knew dinosaurs, but possibly ate them too.

RISE OF THE MAM

On land, the mammals grew and evolved into a whole range of different shapes and sizes. Some were plant-eaters – and others found those plant-eaters very tasty!

Not all ancient mammals were giants; some were smaller versions of animals we know today.

▲ BIGGEST OF ALL

If you think elephants are big, you ain't seen nothing yet! Indricotherium (IN-drik-oh-THEER-ee-um) was the biggest mammal to ever walk the earth. It lived over 25 million years ago and was around 4 metres (13 ft) tall. Luckily for the other land creatures, it was a plant-eater.

BAD CAT ▼

Many carnivorous mammals were cat-like. Thylacosmilus (thy-la-COS-mih-lus) was a marsupial that lived in South America. Its most striking feature was its two huge fangs. It was only outdone by the even bigger sabre-toothed cats.

SURPRISINGLY SMALL ▶

Skeletons of prehistoric dwarf elephants have been found, mostly on islands where food would have been limited. Some were less than a metre tall but they still had big ears.

EARLY HUMANS

You probably know that human beings are distantly related to great apes. What might surprise you is that there were different types of early human, all of which died out apart from our own species – Homo sapiens (HOE-mo SAY-pee-uns).

TOUGH GUYS ▶

A highly successful species of early human was the Neanderthals. They were shorter and stronger than their predecessor Homo heidelbergensis and were good hunters. They were in Europe around 150,000 years before Homo sapiens.

◀ TREE PEOPLE

The oldest human remains were found in Africa. They are nearly 6 million years old. Back then, humans looked a lot like apes and even spent time in trees. More recently, the partial skeleton of a species known as Australopithecus afarensis (oh-stra-lo-PITH-ih-kus A-fa-REN-sis) was found. Nicknamed 'Lucy', it is now thought that 'she' may have been a 'he'. Either way, Lucy is over 3 million years old.

ARTISTS ▶

Homo sapiens have been around for at least 130,000 years. This cave painting demonstrates that our ancestors hunted together, leaving time for art and leisure. Being clever made us adaptable, which is the key for survival.

THE FLORES HOBBIT ▼

When a small skeleton was found on the Indonesian island of Flores it was thought to be a new species. Some scientists now believe it to be a small Homo sapien with a disease that made its brain smaller. You see how difficult this looking at the past can be!

Our human ancestors and near relatives are known as 'hominids'.

WHAT WAS THE ICE

An ice age is when the world's temperature is low for a long period of time and ice spreads out from the poles. Throughout history there have been lots of ice ages, but the one people talk about as *the* Ice Age began around 2.5 million years ago and lasted until about 10,000 years ago.

▲ ICE RETREAT

The Ice Age conjures up images of snow, cold weather and woolly mammoths. It's true that great sheets of ice did cover a lot of the earth's surface; but at times it was quite mild and the ice sheets retreated north.

◄ WHAT CAUSED THE ICE AGE?

As the earth orbits the sun, it can tilt a little, which leads to big changes in temperature. During the last Ice Age, the northern hemisphere of the earth was probably tilted further away from the sun – meaning things got a bit chilly!

AGE?

WHERE DID THEY GO? ▶

The end of the Ice Age was remarkable on two fronts: it got a lot warmer, and a lot of animals disappeared. Were they hunted to extinction? Was it too warm for them? Did the vegetation change too much? No one knows the answer.

Some scientists believe that we are still in the Ice Age but it doesn't feel so cold because we're in one of the warmer periods.

HERE COME THE HUMANS ▶

There were notable developments in the human story during the Ice Age. The Neanderthals were well adapted to the harsh, cold conditions, but when Homo sapiens arrived in Europe about 40,000 years ago, they were in direct competition for food.

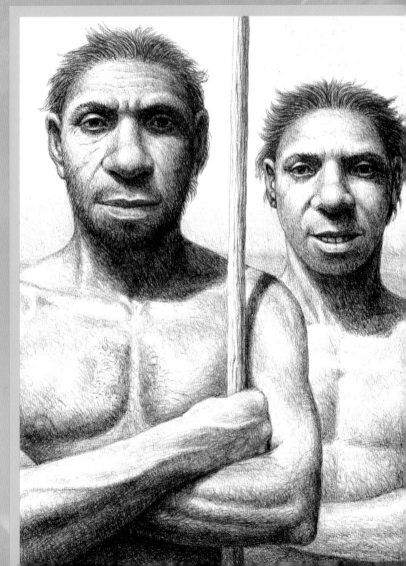

HAIRY BEASTS

If you're out and about in the cold, it is a good idea to wrap up warm. That's precisely what many animals did during the Ice Age. They grew thick shaggy coats to stop themselves freezing to death.

▲ TINY EARS

The mastodon (MASS-toh-don) looked like a mammoth, but was a different species entirely. It had straighter tusks and its teeth were better suited to a diet of tree leaves rather than grass. Like the mammoth, it had small ears.

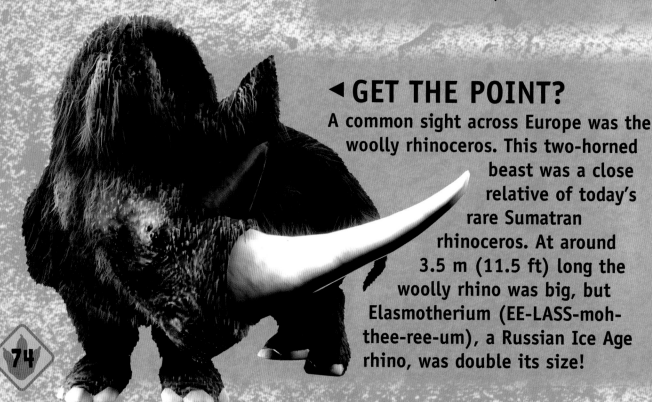

◄ GET THE POINT?

A common sight across Europe was the woolly rhinoceros. This two-horned beast was a close relative of today's rare Sumatran rhinoceros. At around 3.5 m (11.5 ft) long the woolly rhino was big, but Elasmotherium (EE-LASS-moh-thee-ree-um), a Russian Ice Age rhino, was double its size!

◄ WELL ADAPTED

One hairy creature that was particularly well-adapted to the freezing temperatures was the musk ox. Its shaggy coat was ideal in the cold. It was a survivor, too. Its direct relatives are still with us today – but they are over half a metre (1.5 ft) shorter.

Mammoths had a flap of skin that stopped cold air from getting up their bottoms.

◄ SNOW PLOUGH

The most well-known Ice Age animal is the woolly mammoth. There were different kinds of mammoth and not all of them were covered in shaggy fur, but they all had huge, curved tusks. The tusks were probably used to clear snow from the grass so they could eat.

During the Ice Age there were plenty of predators. They were fairly similar to the meat-eaters we have today – but some were much bigger.

SHORT AND LONG

The biggest meat-eater of the Ice Age was the short-faced bear. Its face may have been short, but everything else was huge. It stood at up to 3 m (10 ft) on its hind legs – as tall as a male polar bear. It was possibly a scavenger and may have eaten berries.

◄ SMILEY

The most famous Ice Age carnivore was smilodon (SMY-loh-don), the sabre-toothed tiger. Smilodon wasn't related to today's tigers, but it was just as big and much stockier. Its huge fangs were good for killing but useless for crunching through bone. So no juicy ribs for these cats!

KILLER KITTY ▶

Male African lions can grow to lengths of 2 m (6.5 ft) and can weigh up to 190 kg (420 lbs), but the Ice Age cave lion was a bigger beast altogether. It terrorized the animals of Ice Age Europe.

Male cave lions didn't have manes, which is strange considering how handy they would have been in the cold.

DIRE STRAITS ▶

Another Ice Age predator was the dire wolf. It was larger than a modern-day wolf, but had shorter legs so probably couldn't run as fast. Unfortunately for their prey, dire wolves hunted in packs.

SUPER-SIZED

A feature of the Ice Age period was that many of the animals were a great deal bigger than they are now. Any animal weighing over 44 kg (97 lbs) is classed as being 'megafauna' and the Ice Age had plenty of those. Earth was the land of the giants.

GIANT LUMBERJACK

An Ice Age beaver could grow to the size of a bear! Imagine the size of trees that this toothy terror could chomp its way through!

◄ IRISH GIANT

Even the most impressive antlers on today's stags would look weedy next to those of a Megaloceros (MEH-gah-LOH-seh-rus) or Irish elk. Its antlers could measure over 3.5 m (11.5 ft) across, and the deer itself could be 2 m (6.5 ft) tall. Unfortunately, it also must have been very tasty – it was hunted to extinction around 7,500 years ago.

BOING BOING ▶

Megafauna could be found all around the world. In Australia, there were giant kangaroos, known as Procoptodon (pro-SOP-toh-don). They were twice as tall as today's kangaroos but with shorter faces. They also had a large claw at the end of each foot!

Glyptodon (GLIP-toh-don) was a kind of armadillo that was the size of a small car!

NO SLOTH ▼

Sloths today are slow-moving creatures that spend most of their lives asleep in trees. However, once there were sloths that lived on the ground and some, like Megatherium (MEH-gah-THEER-ee-um), were huge! When Megatherium stood on its back legs it was taller than a grizzly bear.

It's Not Unusual

As the climate during the Ice Age got hotter or colder, the animals would move around to survive. The types of animal living in one area would change accordingly, leading to some surprising results.

▼ GETTING THE HUMP

Camels are usually found in dry and dusty places, but until around 11,000 years ago they also lived in North America! Remains of the now-extinct western camel indicate that it might have looked like a Bactrian (one-humped) camel but it may have had no hump at all.

◄ AHOY THERE!

It was once thought that the first horses arrived in the Americas by boat with the explorers. In a way this is true, as there were no horses on the continent at that time, but horses were there before the Ice Age. They either died out or moved away around 10,000 years ago, possibly due to the changing climate.

JUST LIKE AFRICA ►

If you saw elephants wandering around and a hippopotamus in the river, you would think you were in Africa. But over 120,000 years ago, this would have been an everyday sight across much of Britain!

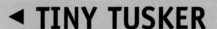

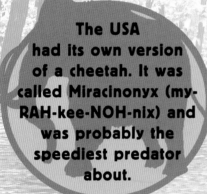

The USA had its own version of a cheetah. It was called Miracinonyx (my-RAH-kee-NOH-nix) and was probably the speediest predator about.

◄ TINY TUSKER

Although many Ice Age animals were bigger than their modern-day counterparts, not all were. A mammoth shorter than an adult human has been found in the Californian Channel Islands in the USA. It seems probable that, as a large species isolated on a small island, it would have had less food to eat so it evolved into a smaller animal to survive.

81

HUMAN BEHAVIOUR

The common image of our ancestors is as grunting, club-wielding cave men, but the people of the Ice Age were smarter than that. Their ability to survive is testament to their intelligence.

THE WINNER IS... ▶

Homo sapiens were taller and slimmer than the Neanderthals. This made them better suited to moving around the newly thawed landscape. They also made finer tools and weapons.

OBSOLETE OR
◀ MURDERED?

Neanderthals disappeared about 28,000 years ago. It was believed that they were unable to adapt to warmer conditions, but new finds dispute this. It now seems likely that they were wiped out by competing Homo sapiens.

GRAFFITI ▶

Our ancestors decorated the walls of caves with their own artwork, often showing hunting scenes and pictures of animals. These cave paintings have been very helpful to scientists and historians, illustrating what life was like during the Ice Age.

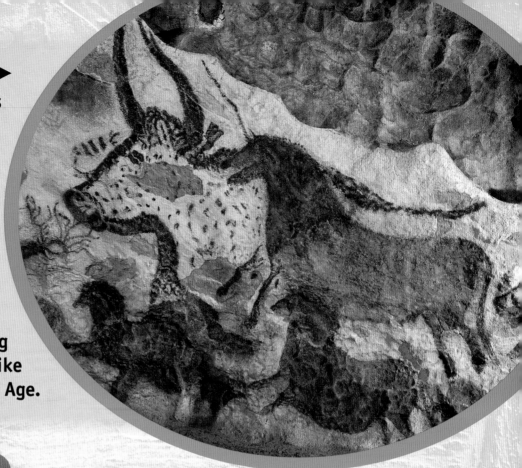

Some scientists believe that modern humans are descended from as few as 10,000 ancient Homo sapiens!

▼ EXTERMINATE

It was long thought that our ancestors were responsible for killing off Ice Age animals. It's true that they did hunt these beasts, but their extinctions could have been due to the changing climate.

LEARNING MORE

Scientists and historians create a picture of the past by studying whatever remains from a particular time. Fortunately, there are lots of remains from the Ice Age, so we have a good idea of how people and animals lived.

BACK FROM THE DEAD

Some mammoth remains are so well-preserved that scientists believe it might be possible to bring mammoths back from extinction. The idea is to cross their DNA with that of their closest living relative, the Indian elephant. Theoretically it is possible, but no one knows if it will work!

STICKY END ▶

Asphalt is a naturally occurring sticky substance, a bit like tar. At Rancho La Brea in the USA, great pools of asphalt have been trapping animals for hundreds of thousands of years. The numerous fossils found are of excellent quality. They include wolves, mammoths and smilodons.

PLANTING EVIDENCE ▶

Across Europe and America there are caves where both people and animals have lived. These caves often provide invaluable information, as they contain bones and samples of pollen. The pollen tells us what kinds of plants were growing at different times.

Scientists know what mammoths ate because they have found the remains of food inside their stomachs.

PERFECTLY ▼ PRESERVED

In the icy Russian tundra, mammoths have been found that are almost perfectly preserved. The cold has kept them frozen in time – just like your freezer keeps your food fresh.

MYTHS AND MONS

F or many years, people have believed that there are still giant reptiles living in the modern world. Even today, some people believe that there are real-life survivors from the age of the dinosaurs.

▼ HERE BE DRAGONS

Fossils of dinosaurs found long ago fuelled the belief in dragons. What else could these huge, unknown skeletons belong to?

Some people believe that the Loch Ness Monster is a plesiosaur that survived to the present day.

TERS

MYSTERY BONES ▼

In the past, strange bones found on beaches were believed to be evidence of sea monsters. They were probably just the carcasses of whales and other large sea animals.

NESSIE ▶

Monster sightings have been reported from lakes all over the world. The most famous is Scotland's Loch Ness Monster. Nessie-spotters claim to have seen a long neck and a humped back gliding through the water.

SEA SERPENTS

The classic sea monster is the sea serpent. There have been reports of gigantic snake-like terrors in seas and lakes for many years.

UNKNOWN TERROR
A large sea serpent nicknamed Chessie is said to live in Chesapeake Bay, USA. A videotape of the creature exists, but the quality is too poor for scientists to tell what Chessie is.

In 1840, a ship's crew thought they'd seen a sea monster. It turned out to be a lump of seaweed!

INLAND SERPENTS ▼
Other famous lake monsters are Ogopogo, said to lurk in Lake Okanagan in Canada, and Champ, from Lake Champlain in the USA.

◄ ENORMOUS FISH

One sea serpent does exist. The oarfish is around 9 m (29 ft) long, with a red dorsal fin running down its body. Could this be the beast that sailors have been spotting for all these years?

FALSE IDENTITY ▼

The anaconda, which lives in rivers in South America, grows to over 9 m (29 ft) long. Could these have inspired stories about sea monsters?

THEN AND NOW

Impressive as they are, the meat-eaters of today would be no match for some of the carnivores of the past. Here are a few of them.

▼MEGA SHARK

Megalodon (MEG-a-lo-don) was a formidable predator. It cruised the oceans until 1.5 million years ago. It was twice the size of a great white shark – it would have eaten one of these for breakfast!

◄ TEAM TACTICS

Ferocious claws and teamwork enabled Deinonychus to take on prey much bigger than itself. Animals such as wolves and lions do the same today, but their prey is not nearly as big!

TERROR BIRD ▶

The sharp beak and claws of the ancient Phorusrhacos (FOR-uss-RAH-cus) tell us that it was a predator capable of ripping and tearing at its prey. At 2.5 m (8 ft) in height, it was as big as a modern ostrich. Some scientists believe it was alive late enough for humans to have seen it!

The largest living bird is the Wandering albatross. With a wingspan of 3.63 m (11 ft), it's tiny compared to Quetzalcoatlus.

MODERN MONSTERS

Dinosaurs, plesiosaurs and pterosaurs may now be extinct, but there are still monsters in our modern world. They might not be as big as their ancient counterparts, but they are scary.

DRAGONS ALIVE

The Komodo dragon is the world's heaviest lizard. A male Komodo dragon can be over 3 m (10 ft) in length. It eats carrion and has knife-like teeth to cut through flesh. Komodos can swim and climb trees, so there is nowhere safe to hide!

GIANT OCTOPUS ▶

The Lusca is a giant octopus that is said to live in the Caribbean. Old photographs of a body washed up on shore suggest that it might actually be real!

REAL-LIFE ▶ MONSTER

The giant squid can grow up to 13 m (43 ft) long. That's the length of a bus!

Whales are often found with sucker marks on their skin from fights with giant squid.

PICTURE CREDITS

AKG: 82 top, 83 bottom.

Ardea London Ltd: 11 bottom, 21 bottom, 32, 33 top, 39 bottom, 40 top, 46 top, 49, 53, 62, 63 bottom.

Bill Stoneham: 12 top, 36 bottom.

Corbis: page 7 bottom, 16 bottom, 23, 30, 35 top, 37 top, 55 bottom, 56, 67 top, 72 bottom, 75 top and bottom, 82 bottom, 87 bottom.

DEA Picture Library: 35 bottom.

Discovery Communications Inc: 34, 87 top.

FLPA: 80 top.

Getty: 2, 9 bottom, 43 top, 76, 81 bottom, 91.

Indiana State Museum and Historic Sites: 77 bottom.

Jon Hughes/Pixelshack: title page, 24, 28, 29 top, 31 bottom, 36 top, 54 bottom.

Natural History Museum: 10, 11 top, 14, 15, 17 bottom, 18 top and bottom, 22, 25 top and bottom, 30 bottom, 38, 40 bottom, 41, 42, 43 bottom, 45 top and bottom, 46 bottom, 47, 49, 51, 52 top and bottom, 57, 63 top, 78, 79.

Nature Picture Library: 44, 48, 88, 93 bottom.

NHPA: 89 bottom.

Oxford Scientific/Photolibrary.com: 59, 60.

Photoshot: 13 bottom, 17 top, 18 bottom, 21 top, 26, 31 top, 54 top, 55 top.

Rex Features: 72 top, 83 top.

Science Photo Library: 6 top left and 39, 6 bottom, 7 top, 12 bottom, 13 middle, 20, 27 top, 33 bottom, 39, 50, 58, 61, 64, 65 top, 66 bottom, 68, 70 top and bottom, 71, 73 bottom, 74 top and bottom, 79, 90 top and bottom, 93 top.

Shropshire County Museum Service: 85 bottom.

Shutterstock: half-title page, icon images pages 8–94, 5, 8, 9 top, 27 bottom, 65 bottom, 66 top, 71 top, 73 top, 77 top, 80 bottom, 81 top, 85 top, 86, 92, 95 top and bottom.

Topfoto: 67 bottom, 84, 89 top.

Wikimedia: 69 bottom.

Cover: Shutterstock.

Every effort has been made to clear copyright. Should there be any inadvertent omission, please apply to the publisher for rectification.

GIANT OCTOPUS ▶

The Lusca is a giant octopus that is said to live in the Caribbean. Old photographs of a body washed up on shore suggest that it might actually be real!

REAL-LIFE ▶ MONSTER

The giant squid can grow up to 13 m (43 ft) long. That's the length of a bus!

Whales are often found with sucker marks on their skin from fights with giant squid.

GLOSSARY

Absorb
To soak up

Amphibian
A cold-blooded animal that often lives on land but breeds in water, such as a frog or newt

Asteroid
A space rock that enters earth's atmosphere

Atmosphere
The layer of gases that surround the earth

Bacteria
Single-celled organisms that can only been seen through a microscope

Carcasses
The bodies of dead animals

Carrion
The rotting flesh of dead animals

Continent
Any one of the seven unbroken landmasses on earth

Descendant
A person, animal or species that is related to a previous person, animal or species

Diverge
To split or go in different directions

Diversify
To spread out and become more varied

Evolve
To change over a long period of time

Fossil
The remains of a prehistoric plant or animal found in rocks

Mammal
A warm-blooded animal that produces milk for its young, such as humans, cats and whales

Marsupial
A type of mammal that has a pouch in which its babies continue to grow

Orbit
The path that a planet, moon or comet takes around another planet or star, such as the sun

Palaeontology
The study of fossils and prehistoric life

Predator
An animal that catches, kills and eats other animals

Prehistoric
The period of human history before people started to make records and write things down

Prey
An animal hunted, caught and eaten by another animal

Prising
Opening with force

Reign
The period when a king or queen rules

Reptile
A cold-blooded, usually scaly, animal that lays eggs

Scavenger
An animal that feeds on whatever it can find, including animals killed by another meat-eater

Species
A group of animals that are similar to each other and can breed with one another, such as dogs. Species can be further split into different varieties, such as greyhounds or poodles.

PICTURE CREDITS

AKG: 82 top, 83 bottom.

Ardea London Ltd: 11 bottom, 21 bottom, 32, 33 top, 39 bottom, 40 top, 46 top, 49, 53, 62, 63 bottom.

Bill Stoneham: 12 top, 36 bottom.

Corbis: page 7 bottom, 16 bottom, 23, 30, 35 top, 37 top, 55 bottom, 56, 67 top, 72 bottom, 75 top and bottom, 82 bottom, 87 bottom.

DEA Picture Library: 35 bottom.

Discovery Communications Inc: 34, 87 top.

FLPA: 80 top.

Getty: 2, 9 bottom, 43 top, 76, 81 bottom, 91.

Indiana State Museum and Historic Sites: 77 bottom.

Jon Hughes/Pixelshack: title page, 24, 28, 29 top, 31 bottom, 36 top, 54 bottom.

Natural History Museum: 10, 11 top, 14, 15, 17 bottom, 18 top and bottom, 22, 25 top and bottom, 30 bottom, 38, 40 bottom, 41, 42, 43 bottom, 45 top and bottom, 46 bottom, 47, 49, 51, 52 top and bottom, 57, 63 top, 78, 79.

Nature Picture Library: 44, 48, 88, 93 bottom.

NHPA: 89 bottom.

Oxford Scientific/Photolibrary.com: 59, 60.

Photoshot: 13 bottom, 17 top, 18 bottom, 21 top, 26, 31 top, 54 top, 55 top.

Rex Features: 72 top, 83 top.

Science Photo Library: 6 top left and 39, 6 bottom, 7 top, 12 bottom, 13 middle, 20, 27 top, 33 bottom, 39, 50, 58, 61, 64, 65 top, 66 bottom, 68, 70 top and bottom, 71, 73 bottom, 74 top and bottom, 79, 90 top and bottom, 93 top.

Shropshire County Museum Service: 85 bottom.

Shutterstock: half-title page, icon images pages 8–94, 5, 8, 9 top, 27 bottom, 65 bottom, 66 top, 71 top, 73 top, 77 top, 80 bottom, 81 top, 85 top, 86, 92, 95 top and bottom.

Topfoto: 67 bottom, 84, 89 top.

Wikimedia: 69 bottom.

Cover: Shutterstock.

Every effort has been made to clear copyright. Should there be any inadvertent omission, please apply to the publisher for rectification.